Ex libris

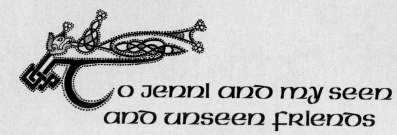

To Jenni and my seen
and unseen friends

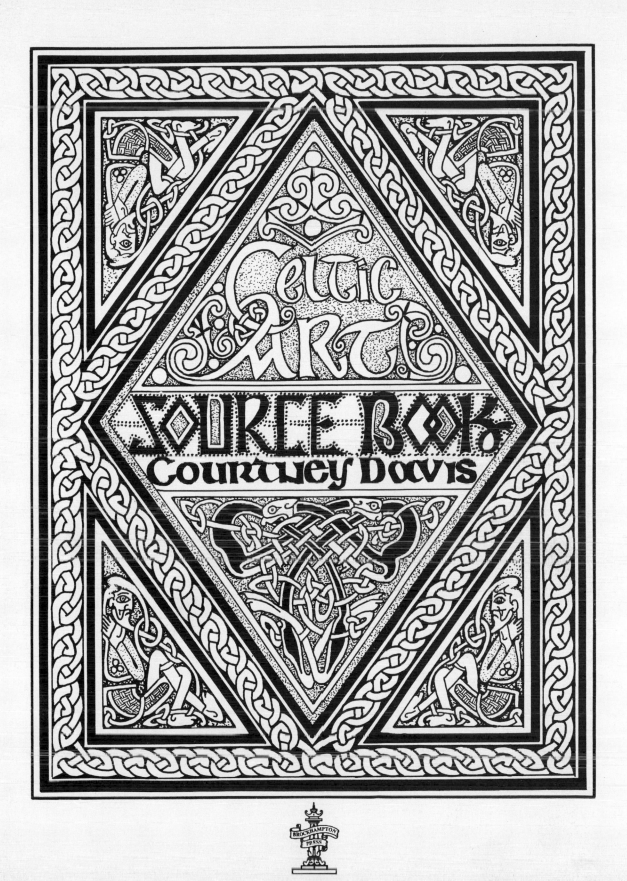

Celtic Art
Source Book

Courtney Davis

Brockhampton Press

Blandford Press
A Cassell Imprint

Cassell Illustrated 2-4 Heron Quays London E14 4JP

Text and illustrations copyright © Courtney Davis 1988

First published in Great Britain 1988
Reprinted 1989
Reprinted 1990
Reprinted 1994
Paperback edition first published in Great Britain 1989
Reprinted 1990 (twice), 1991 (twice), 1992, 1993, 1994 (twice), 1995, 1996 (twice)

This edition Published 1999 by Brockhampton Press
An imprint of the Caxton Publishing Group
Reprinted 2003
ISBN 1 86019 8589

British Library Cataloguing in Publication Data
Davis, Courtney, *1946-*
    The Celtic art source book.
    1. Great Britain. Celtic visual arts
    I. Title
    709',01'4

Designed by Courtney Davis
Typeset in Hong Kong by Asco Trade Typesetting Ltd

Printed at Oriental Press, Dubai, U.A.E.

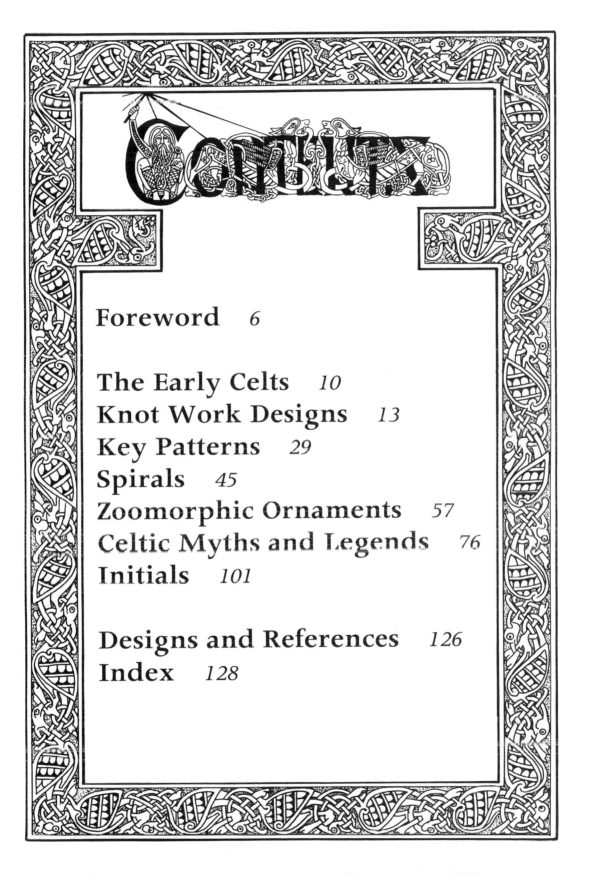

Contents

FOREWORD
By Johan H. Quanjer

Symbolism and the Mystical Experience – The soul in communion with the cosmos.
'In a symbol lies concealment or revelation'.

Thomas Carlyle (1795–1881)

The art of understanding symbols and symbolism is once again gripping the imagination of mankind. The Greek word symbol means that which is thrown or brought together and is the opposite of diabolical which means thrown apart or separated.

A symbol represents an image which links us to the higher levels of subjective intuitive experience as well as to our conscious immediate awareness. It is a midway point between what is 'out there' and what is deeply embedded within.

The art of symbology was understood and practised for many thousands of years until about 300 years ago, when the French mathematician and philosopher René Descartes separated spirituality from materialism, and it fell into disuse. However, since the last century we have gradually begun to revive this forgotten language of symbolism. With the advent of the world-wide Consciousness Movement in recent times, renewed interest has been shown by many people, some of whom have become aware of the impact a symbol can have on our psyche to improve our well-being.

Through symbolism we can see the soul of man awakening to the realisation of his true purpose, leading him to a higher level of conscious awareness. The novice is often unaware that we are surrounded everywhere by symbols, the most obvious one being the sun. This is an ancient universal symbol of light. On the physical level it is the bringer of life to this planet, the force that creates, stimulates, renews and heals. On a spiritual level it represents the solar logos – the word of God, the representative of the godhead for our solar system. In view of this it may not have been such a pagan or unchristian act for the Pharaoh Akhenaton (among others) to have worshipped the sun, for he would have recognised the solar logos behind it which would have connected him to the god quality within himself. As a result the sun became that mystical symbol which united him with his higher mystical qualities and possibilities. In this way the symbol can aid us in our mystical experience, help develop a deep intuitive awareness of all we survey and, as such, act as transformer.

Another great symbol is water. The Babylonians called the sea the home of wisdom. It symbolises a great mysterious immensity from which everything comes and into which everything returns. It also represents the wisdom and intuitive feminine aspects of our being. Merlin can also be seen and is often understood as the man from the sea – that is, our essential link with the cosmic sea, our higher ideals.

Merlin as a symbol has lost his image of an outside being, a bearded wizard, and is beginning to speak to us within ourselves as our intuitive self. With this intuitive Merlin aspect awakened in us, we can tune in to the cosmos and become aware of our cosmic origins on a level which will help free us from material bondage (if we are not already free) and accept eternal values.

It is said that Merlin was imprisoned in a tree and is now awakening to liberation. This represents our higher intuitive awareness trying to find release from gross materialism.

In symbolism everything has some meaning and a purpose. We should therefore be cognisant of what forces we are tuning in to when contemplating a particular symbol or when we have it as a base for meditation. Whereas the symbol is most often linked to ancient archetypal patterns or images this does not preclude us from going on our own mystical journeyings as reflected from our level of awareness. In other words there is no definitive hard and fast rule which each image must represent. For instance, in essence the Grail enfolds two main symbols – that of the Cup or Chalice, and that of the Quest. But whichever way we look at it, the Grail is perceived as a source of illumination. The Grail or Cup has also been interpreted as the Third Eye, represent-

ing our inwardly perceived sense of eternity. The loss of the Grail was therefore tantamount to the loss of our inner source of fulfilment and joy; hence the 'unending' search.

In the past this search was always external and many an expedition was mounted to find a richly bejewelled cup of great value. In the present day it is seen as an inner search, an inner journey we must all take, and while beset by danger and doubt, fear and loss of faith, we eventually recognise the Grail within our own being to show the way to self-realisation and self-awareness.

Although we may think we are trying to find joy and fulfilment, what we are truly searching for may be a further awareness beyond human comprehension. And the study of symbolism may lead us to make discoveries the glory of which we may only dimly perceive in our most inspired moments as yet.

When we experience the symbol as the gateway to higher thinking and living, we become aware that we have transcended the personality and touched deeply on our soul quality. We then recognise that it is through the self or soul that we make an inner contact with the godhead, on a level beyond reason or intellect. Furthermore we accept that we are part of the whole and that the whole is part of us. By this touch of the soul we are harmonised, vivified and recharged with energy. We are imbued with the certainty of the saint and the faith of the Apostle and are so renewed and ready to go back to the area of our personal lives and meet any of its emergencies and challenges with courage and joy.

The symbol has no power of its own; it is only what it *represents* that exerts an influence. We should not be forever bound to it, for once we have begun to become self-actualised individuals the need for symbolism will disappear. However, if we remove symbols before we have risen in consciousness, we may cut ourselves off from that source which enables us to achieve cosmic awareness.

In business, symbols are often manufactured in design studios with little or no knowledge of the science behind them. And when the designer is oblivious of the symbol's magnetic attraction, he or she may produce an image which is contrary to the firm's interests.

A powerful symbol is one that attracts beneficent energies for the growth and stimulation of the company and the people working in it. This may also count for an entire nation or a confederation of nations who are linked to a particular State symbol.

I hope that this book will set you on your own personal Quest and help you discover the meanings of symbols and symbolism in your own way. They are part of our rich cultural heritage to take us forward on an upward and ever more outward direction into eternity.

Johan H. Quanjer, Battersea, London, 1988

CELTIC

A JOURNEY THROUGH THE ROMANTIC REALMS OF CELTIC ART

The Early Celts

Early Decorative and Religious Art

Celtic art displays a richness of colour, intricacy and symbolism to equal that of the world's finest styles of religious art. It was born of the Druidic religion and the oral traditions of the Celtic people, especially those who inhabited Britain and Ireland from the seventh century BC.

The Celtic artist worked with stone, wood, metal and paint in a style characterised by its abstract nature, balance of form, delicacy, brightness of colour, and most of all by its spirals and interlacings.

Prior to the advent of Christianity in Britain, this style was applied in three main areas:

(a) in carvings on stone monuments for magical purposes, such as the aversion of evil, and for use in Druidic ceremonies;

(b) in the fashioning of fine metal jewellery and gear, and the firing of bright enamels, to adorn the Celtic warrior, his horse and chariot;

(c) in warpaint, which featured symbols in blue woad.

The seven created beings of the Celtic world – plant, insect, fish, reptile, bird, mammal and man – are all featured in the artwork. But because the copying or portrayal of the works of the creator was forbidden, the artist's representation of natural creatures is highly stylised and abstracted; arms, legs, hair and beard are intertwined in intricate patterns.

Like their pagan gods and spirits, the Druids themselves are said to have practised shape-changing, so it is not unusual to find their gods portrayed as having bird or animal servants, or even bird or animal body parts. This same characteristic was later incorporated into the Christian Gospels, where the evangelists are given both animal and human forms.

A standing stone at Glencolumbcille, Co. Donegal, Ireland

Materials

The original artists had a variety of coloured pigments from many sources at their disposal. Colours such as ultramarine came from as far as the foothills of the Himalayas, and kermes (red) was obtained from insects living in the evergreen trees of the Mediterranean lands. Gold and silver, however, were rarely used by the scribes; for example, gold only appears three times in the Lindisfarne Gospels, in very small patches. All the colours were ground by the artist and bound with egg white (albumen), fish glue or natural gum.

There is little evidence concerning the types of pens, brushes, tools or aids to eyesight that enabled the Celts to paint and draw with an exactness which is difficult for the modern artist to copy, even with today's technology. Professor J. O. Westwood wrote:

'In the space of about a quarter of an inch superficial, I counted with magnifying glass no less than 158 interlacements of a slender ribbon pattern formed of white lines edged with black ones, upon a black ground. No wonder tradition should allege that these unerring lines should have been traced by angels'. (*Celtic Art: The Methods of Construction*)

In all their work, the Celtic artists were inspired by the supreme perfection of God. To show humility, an artist would deliberately leave parts unfinished so as to avoid the possibility of absolute perfection in his personal endeavour.

Saints built into the twelfth century church wall,
White Island, Co. Fermanagh, Ireland

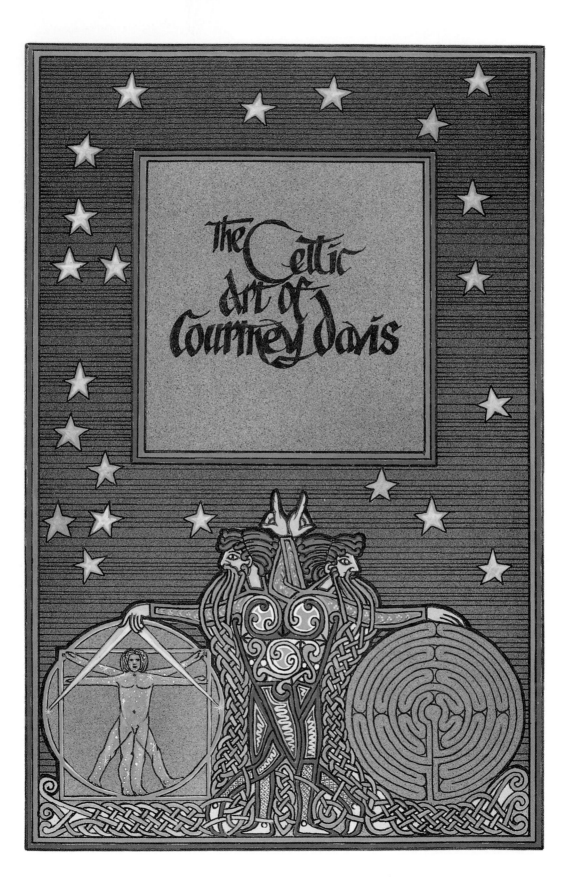

The Celtic Art of Courtney Davis

Design adapted from stencilled decorations
of 1920–30 in an oratory of the Dominican convent, Dunloagmaire,
Co. Dublin (Sister Concepta Lynch O.P.)

KNOT WORK DESIGNS

The Thread of Life

The human soul, it is believed, is a fragment of the divine, and will ultimately return to its divine source. Through successive rebirths the soul rids itself of its accumulated, inherited impurities, until it finally achieves the goal of perfection.

The interlaced knot work patterns with their unbroken lines, symbolise the process of man's eternal spiritual growth. When the cord is unravelled, it leads us on — an aid to concentration occupying the conscious mind with a demanding, repetitive task. Similarly, one might use a mantra or rosary beads to reach the heart of our nature.

the celtic knot

19

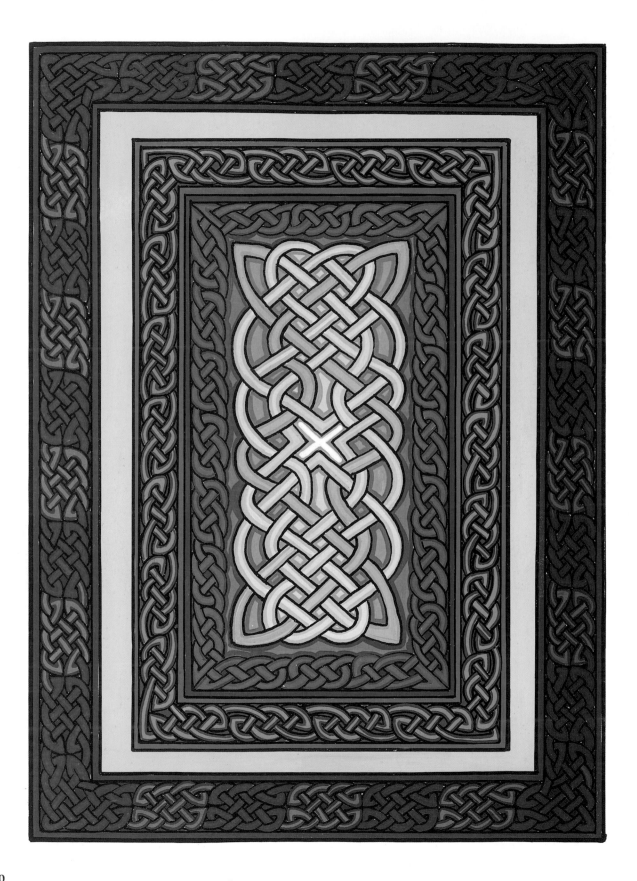

Inner
contemplation

22

23

the unbroken
rhythms of the past

the sacred
thread of life

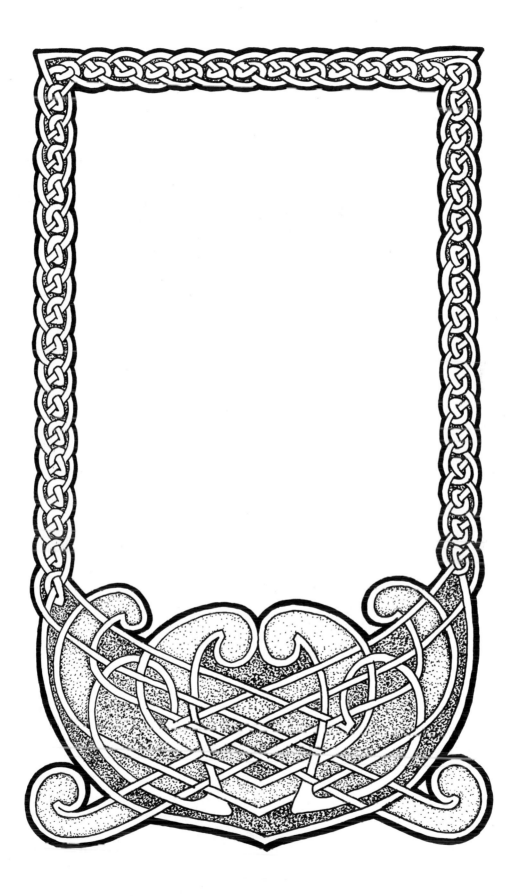

Lifespirit

KEY PATTERNS

KEY PATTERNS

The Sacred Dance

Key and step patterns are really spirals in straight lines.
When connected, they become a processional path,
leading through a complex maze to the sacred *omphalos*
at the centre – the point where Heaven and Earth are
joined.

Labyrinths, like wells, were primarily religious objects
and were incorporated into the Christian church. On the
solar celebrations and other religious festivals, the adept
danced the 'Sacred Dance' barefoot to absorb the earth's
energies, through the Labyrinth. This was a journey
through progressive levels of experience, physical, mental
and spiritual, until the vortex at the centre was reached.
In Christian times, this journey was said to be the spiritual equivalent of a pilgrimage to Jerusalem.

31

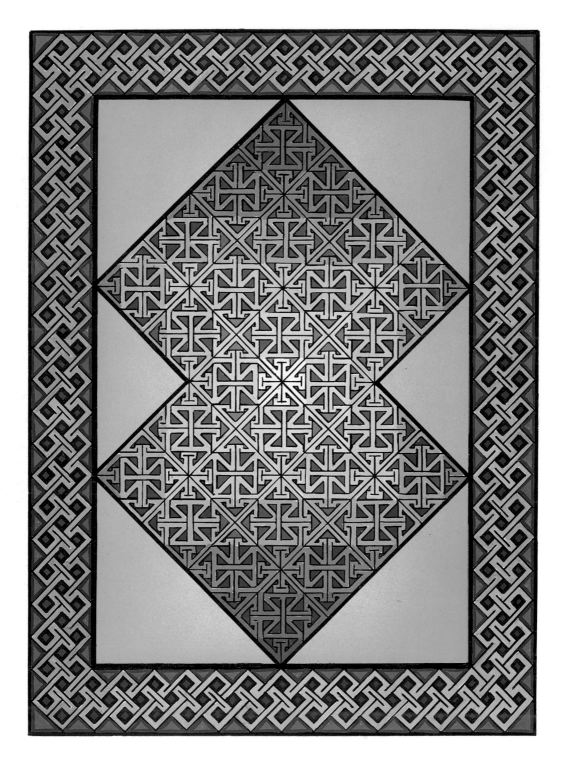

JOURNEY
OF THE INITIATE

REBIRTH

the Labyrinth
to the omphalos

the mystic
transformation

vesica piscis

the INNer Quest

43

Gateway to Infinity

SPIRALS

The Cosmic Symbol

The spiral is the natural form of growth. In every culture past and present it has become a symbol of eternal life. Surrounded by water as they worked, the Celtic monks were reminded constantly of the flow and movement of the cosmos. The whorls they painted represented the continuous creation and dissolution of the world; the passages between the spirals symbolised the divisions between life, death and rebirth. In the Neolithic world, passing a spiral barrier (see the design below) into an inner sanctuary seems to have been a necessary passport in the journey of the sacred dance through the labyrinth to the sacred realms beyond the centre. The labyrinth creates and protects the still centre, allowing entry to its knowledge only in the correct way, through initiation. Before the knowledge can be imparted, old preconceptions must be discarded and the traveller must re-enter the preformal state of the womb. At the centre, there is complete balance: the point where Heaven and Earth are joined. The descending gyre of Heaven is the materialisation of spirit into matter, maintaining a state of balance, in the initiate inwardly and outwardly — in a state of perfect being.

In the sacred dance, we mirror the macrocosmic order of the heavens, the gyratory movement representing the whirling of the stars above the fixed earth. As we wind, we create within ourselves a still centre and apprehend the being of the universe into being; as we unwind, we turn our spirit back to its divine source.

The spiral-marked entrance stone blocking the entrance to Newgrange megalithic tomb, Co. Meath, Ireland

47

the inner spirals

celtic cross

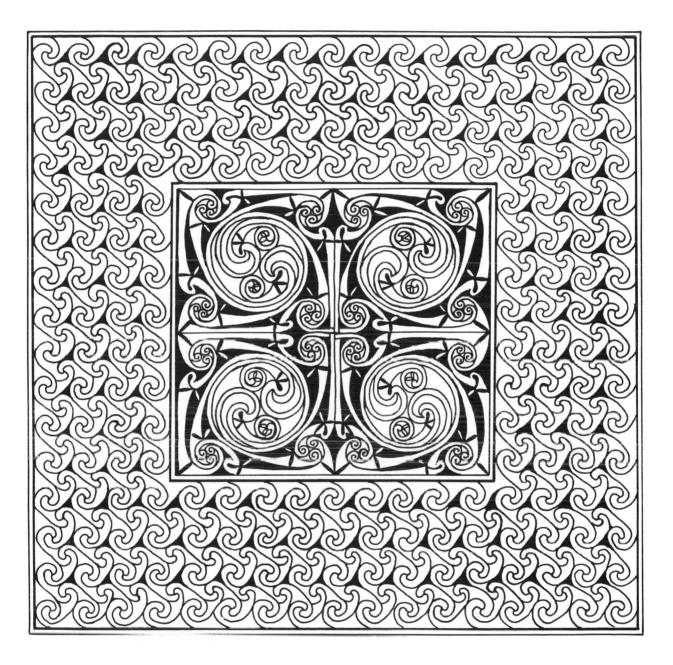

omphalos

the oracle

May your
cup overflow
with health
and happiness
this yule
time.

the christmas cup

ZOOMORPHIC ORNAMENTS

The animals and birds were sacred to the Celts and many of their gods and spirits are represented with bird or animal parts. Shape-shifting, or changing of form, was said to have been used by the Druids and the deities in the early legends, and by semi-mythological characters who adopted the form of an animal.

Zoomorphics and anthropomorphic ornaments show us that nothing is as it first appears; plants turn into tails, and, inter-weaving, develop a head, legs or feet. These intricate patterns first appeared in the Bronze Age art of Britain and Ireland. The craftsmen fashioned them into a complicated contortion of bodies, but they kept the motif still logical and conforming with nature.

In the *Book of Kells*, this influence is emphasised by repeatedly depicting the four evangelists through their symbols: the man for Matthew, the lion for Mark, the calf for Luke and the eagle for John, although they were also depicted in fairly natural forms. Neither is it unusual for animals to appear with hands and human feet, or even to see a calf's head on an eagle's body.

the celtic experience

THE MYSTIC SPIRAL

63

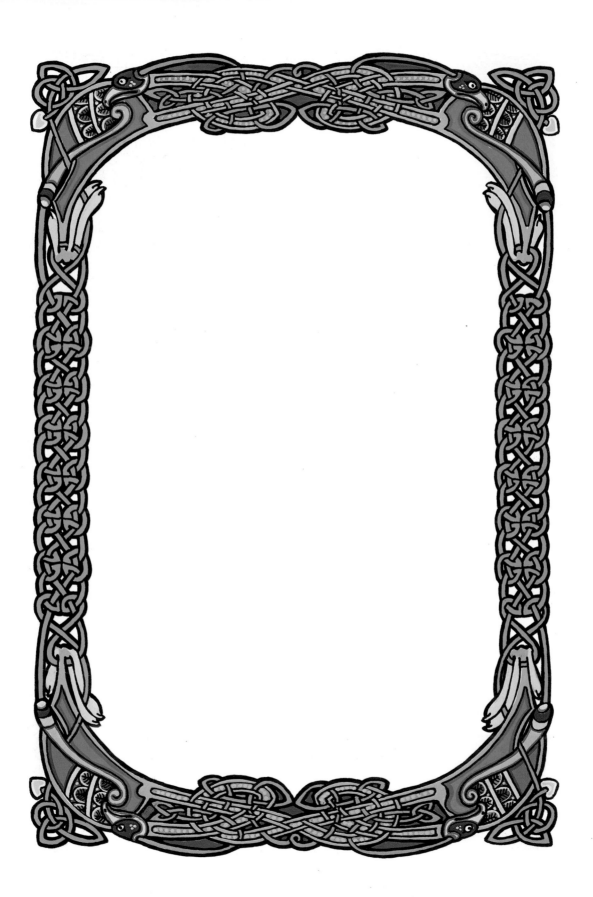

the great spirit

Cover design for a record album by Michael Law

xcalibur

© COURTNEY DAVIS 1986

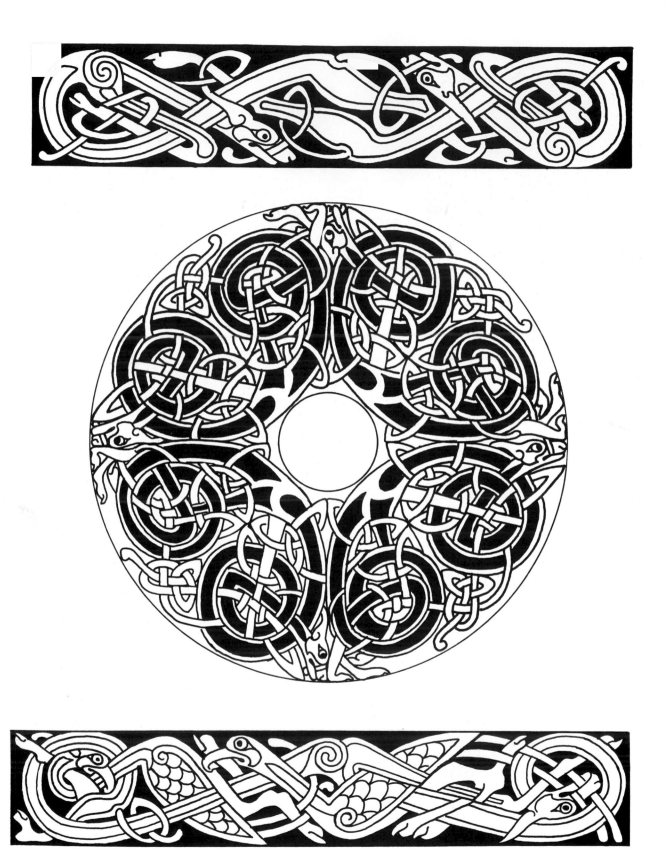

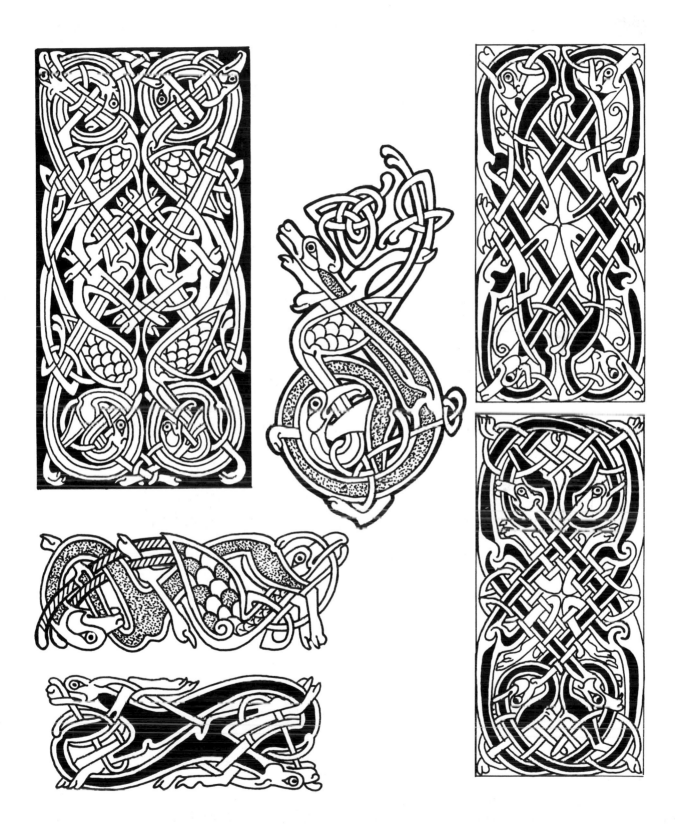

Celtic Myths and Legends

St Brendan from a design by Harry Clarke around 1916, taken from a stained glass window in Honan Chapel, Cork

st columba

SAINT COLUMBA

Born about the year 521 in Donegal, St Columba was the most important of the missionary saints. He was a direct descendant of King Niall, and a cousin of the King who by then ruled over north-west Ireland. Determined to become a priest he studied at several monastic schools, and also learned the older skills of poetry from the bardic schools. In later life he would defend the poets when the Church and Kings sought to do away with the relics of the Irish past.

As an Irish prince Columba had great influence; and though he seems to have been generous and humane, he was also a very forceful person. He was very active in establishing monasteries such as Durrow, Kells and Swords and the Lonely Tory island off the Donegal coast.

About AD 560 Columba quarrelled with a fellow abbot over a book, which still exists in Dublin. He accused St Columba of copying the book without permission, and claimed that the copy belonged to him by right. The High King of Tara supported this selfish attitude and in his fury Columba collected together his supporters. On the slopes of Ben Bulben they did battle against the High King, who was eventually killed.

Either because he was ashamed of his part in the quarrel, or because of his missionary zeal, Columba set off for Scotland in the year 563. He established the famous monastery on Iona, which like many monasteries in Ireland soon attracted students and became a great centre of learning. On one journey to meet the hostile King of the Picts, he encountered the Loch Ness monster, which unwisely attempted to swallow one of his followers. Columba spoke so forcefully that it seems to have been hiding almost ever since.

In time, Celtic churches, high crosses and monastery walls spread over the western parts of Scotland. In the lands of the Picts, the faith took hold more slowly, and though many small monasteries were founded, little is known of them.

Eventually, the Christian cross began to appear on the stone monuments of the Picts, and little stone churches, even round towers similar to those of Ireland, spread throughout eastern Scotland.

Four priests wearing hooded cloaks, some carrying book satchels, eighth century, Shetland Isles

THE CHILDREN OF LIR

A powerful Irish chieftain named Lir had married the eldest of three
beautiful maidens, and in the course of time they had four fair children—
a daughter and three sons. The mother died when the children were very
young, and Lir married again. His new wife Eva was very beautiful but,
though no one knew it, she was a sorceress. Jealous of her husband's love
of his children, she plotted to destroy them.

At first she tried to bribe her servants to put them to death. As they
refused, she was forced to do the deed herself. But seeing the children
playing happily, she was unable to bring herself to do the wicked deed.
Instead, she persuaded an ancient Druid who lived in a nearby cave to
put an enchantment on the children in order to obtain her wish. The
Druid told her to call the children and persuade them to bathe in Lake
Dairbreak, to cool and refresh them after their playing.

As the waters covered them, the magic spells of Eva and the Druid
changed them into four beautiful white swans.

'Birds shall ye be', chanted the Druid from the bank as the change took
place, 'until you hear the voice of a Christian bell'.

On seeing the result of the spell, Eva was afraid to face her husband,
and repented utterly of her evil deed. As punishment, the King pro-
nounced that she should turn into a demon of the air until the end of
time.

Hundreds of years passed; then one soft spring morning the swans
heard the sound of a Christian bell as they floated on Lake Dairbreak.
For St Patrick had come to Ireland and everywhere men were building
churches. With the sound of the distant bell, the spell was broken, and
the children of Lir returned to their own shapes. But they had lived so
long that, after they had learned the Christian faith, they were glad to
lie down and rest forever, and were all buried in the self-same tomb.

The Children of Lir

"Birds shall Se Se"

the silver branch

THE VOYAGE OF BRAN

Written as early as the eighth century, the theme of the story is well known in Irish literature. Bran, the hero, was out one day walking near his home when he heard sweet music, which sent him to sleep. He awoke to find beside him a silver branch covered with white flowers. On returning to his house, a strange woman appeared and sang of the wonders of the Otherworld: so enchanting was her song that Bran was persuaded to visit the place. As she left him, the magic silver branch sprang from his hand and into the woman's. Bran and twenty-seven companions set out to search for this enchanted world.

Bran met Mannanán mac Lir, the sea god, driving his chariot on the waves as if over a flowery plain. The god chanted verses to Bran in which he prophesied the coming of Christ, and how he would beget a son, Morgan, a reincarnation of the divine hero Finn MacCumaill.

Many years passed, but to the wanderers in the Otherworld it was but a brief span of time. Eventually one of the travellers yearned for the sight of Ireland again, and they decided to return. On reaching the shore, the homesick man leapt from the boat and on touching the soil of Ireland, became a pile of ashes. Bran told the gathered welcoming crowds about the wonders of the Otherworld before returning with his men to the enchanted land, never to return.

Sacred Wells and Springs

Water is a fundamental necessity of life, so it is natural that a visible source of water should be held in special reverence.

Apart from their life-giving properties, springs were claimed to help fertility, cure illness, and provide the gift of prophecy. At certain times of the year it was believed that the spirit of the springs could be invoked to achieve the desired results: fertility, health and knowledge of the future. The Christian church drew wells and springs into its influence, so that they would not remain centres of the old religion, but the old uses were still to continue even though many wells now bore the names of Christian saints. Their sanctity was still rooted in an earlier religion of nature.

The Magic Kiss

One day Niall, son of Eochu Muigmedon, King of Ireland, was hunting with his four brothers when he came across a hideous old woman guarding a well.

The old tale tells us that 'She was as black as coal. Her hair was like a wild horse's tail. Her foul teeth were visible from ear to ear and were such as would sever a branch of green oak. Her eyes were black, her nose crooked and spread. Her body was scrawny, spotted and diseased. Her shins were bent. Her knees and ankles were thick, her shoulders broad, her nails were green'.

As a price for the water from the well, the hag demanded a kiss from each of the brothers in turn. Only Niall overcame his revulsion and kissed her, whereupon she turned into a beautiful woman.

niall and the old hag

The King

Arthur

The earliest information about Arthur is to be found in the eleventh-century collection of Welsh romantic stories called the *Mabinogion*. This recounts the tales of a great hero who rid the land of giants, monsters and witches by super-human feats, similar to the labours of the Greek hero Hercules.

In the Welsh poem *The Spoils of Annwn* he sails in his ship Prydwen to the land of the dead to seize the Magic Cauldron of Annwn, from which only the brave and true could eat. This cauldron may be the original Holy Grail, and if it supplied the food of immortal heroes, then Arthur may have gained immortality by seizing it.

In the early Celtic stories, Arthur has a large band of heroic companions whose names bear a close similarity to those of the later Knights of the Round Table, including his wife Gwenhwyfar (Guinevere).

Many believe that the eighteen-acre site of Cadbury Castle in Somerset is the location of the Arthurian Court of Camelot. It is said that on each Midsummer's Eve, there, Arthur leads his knights along the causeway that links the village of North Barrow and South Barrow. Tradition also has it that Arthur sleeps beneath the fortifications, in a cave with his knights waiting for the time when he will awaken once again to serve Britain.

Warrior on horseback, from a north German gravestone of about AD 700

Joseph of Arimathea

Oral traditions of Somerset, Gloucester and the west of Ireland tell us that the New Testament character Joseph of Arimathea, as a metal merchant, traded with the tin miners of Cornwall and Somerset, and that on one of his visits he brought the boy Jesus with him. It is thought that William Blake was inspired by these tales to write his famous hymn *Jerusalem*, with the line, 'And did those feet in ancient time/Walk upon England's mountains green'.

Jesus' reputed stay lasted a winter. In this time, using skills learned from his earthly father Joseph, he helped to erect the first church in Britain, at Glastonbury, known as Ealde Chiche or the 'Old Church'. St Augustine wrote to Pope Gregory the Great speaking of the first followers of Christ: 'God beforehand aquainting them, found a church constructed by no human art, but by the hands of Christ Himself for the salvation of His people'.

In AD 37, four years after the crucifixion, St Phillip called on Joseph of Arimathea to carry the new religion to Britain. In *A little monument to the once famous Abbey and Borough of Glastonbury*, a collection of local folktales published in 1714, the antiquary Eyston wrote:

> 'St Joseph of Arimathea landed not far from the town, at a place where there was an oak planted in memory of his landing, called 'The Oak of Avalon', that he and his companions marched thence to a hill, near a mile on the south side of the town, and there being weary rested themselves, which gave the hill the name Wearyall Hill, that St Joseph stuck on the hill his staff, being a dry hawthorn stick, which grew and constantly budded and bloomed on Christmas Day'.

Up until recent times people gathered on the old Christmas Eve, 5 January, to watch the Glastonbury Thorn come into flower. Joseph and his followers settled in Glastonbury as hermits, erecting around the Old Church a larger structure as a place to live and worship. This became the foundation for Glastonbury Abbey, the burial place of saints and kings. With him, Joseph brought the cup that was used at the Last Supper, known as the Holy Grail, which is said to have been buried by him in Glastonbury beneath Chalice Hill.

Joseph and The Holy Cup

*Glastonbury, in Somerset, England, incorporating legends
and symbols associated with it*

Glastonbury

The place now known as Glastonbury in Somerset has at different points in its history also been called *Ynnis-witryn* or the Crystal Isle, and the Isle of Avalon; these names give some indication of the mystical and magical qualities which have been attributed to it over the years.

One of its strongest and most enduring identities has been that of a portal linking Heaven and Earth, and from long before Celtic times up to the present it has been used as a spiritual centre.

The winding path which is an unmistakable feature of Glastonbury Tor is a three-dimensional maze which represents the energy that flows through the earth along ley lines. On the appropriate days, walking the maze invokes the power of the Serpent, symbol of knowledge and energy.

A less familiar feature is the ten-mile-wide Glastonbury Zodiac, allegedly constructed on the advice of Merlin the Magician. It was formed by modifying ancient earthworks, roads and dykes to depict the old signs of the zodiac. Lost for years in the changing face of Glastonbury, it was rediscovered in the 1920s by Katherine Maltwood. She saw a cryptic reflection of the Arthurian legend laid out in the earth around Avalon: the round table was the zodiac, the knights and their opponents were metaphors for cosmic patterns and bodies. The pure seeker of the Grail on the path of development would pass through each of the zodiac's twelve doors, assuming and experiencing through numerous incarnations the characteristic features of each of the twelve signs. Finally, at the Tor itself, the seeker reached the sign of Aquarius, the ancient representation of the phoenix drinking the blood of Jesus from the Grail. Upon reaching this symbol of resurrection, the seeker rediscovered the Kingdom and came to rest.

ARTHURUS REX
QUONDAM REXQUE
FUTURUS.

The Birds of Peace and the Serpents of Knowledge

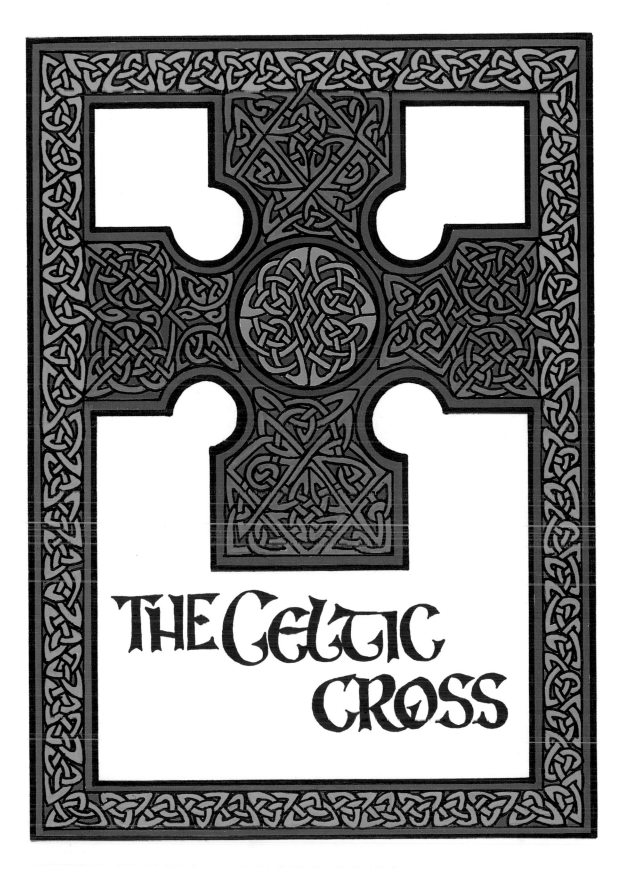

THE CELTIC CROSS

The Cross

Although the cross is best known as the supreme symbol of the Christian faith, cross symbolism itself is much older than Christianity. The oldest examples are those engraved or painted on flat pebbles, dating from 10,000 BC, found in a cave in the French Pyrenees. These 'ancestor stones' were believed to contain the spirits of the dead.

The cross symbolises the four roads; it is derived from quartering the circle through the omphalos at the centre. The cross in the wheel has been used as a symbol for the Sun, and Christ's rule over all things – length, breadth, height and depth.

Knotwork Cross

*The Aberlemno Stone with the seven spirals at the centre
showing the inner stillness within all of us*

Jesus the Archdruid

The introduction of Christianity to Britain and Ireland from the fifth century AD onwards did not signal the abandonment of the Druidic religion. Indeed, Christianity was regarded as the fulfilment of Druidism for Saint Columba himself spoke of Jesus as the 'Archdruid'. By the sixth century, Pope Gregory permitted a fusion of Christian and Celtic beliefs which rendered an easier acceptance of the new without destroying the old. The former Druidic sites such as pools, springs, wells, groves, clearings and standing stones became the new foundation for the Celtic Church.

With the spread of Christianity, the four Gospels documenting the life and teachings of Christ needed to be duplicated, and the Christian missionaries called upon the same artisans who had worked for the pagan chieftains to decorate the Gospels. Only a highly esteemed artist would be charged with the execution of such an important task, and his preparation would be undertaken with great care. During a period of fasting and meditation he would attempt to visualise the complete work, keeping in mind that the manuscripts were to be used in church ceremonies and carried in processions. Their purpose was to offer people a visual symbol that would enshrine the Word of God.

Initial page at the beginning of St Jerome's letter to Pope Damasus in the Lindisfarne Gospels

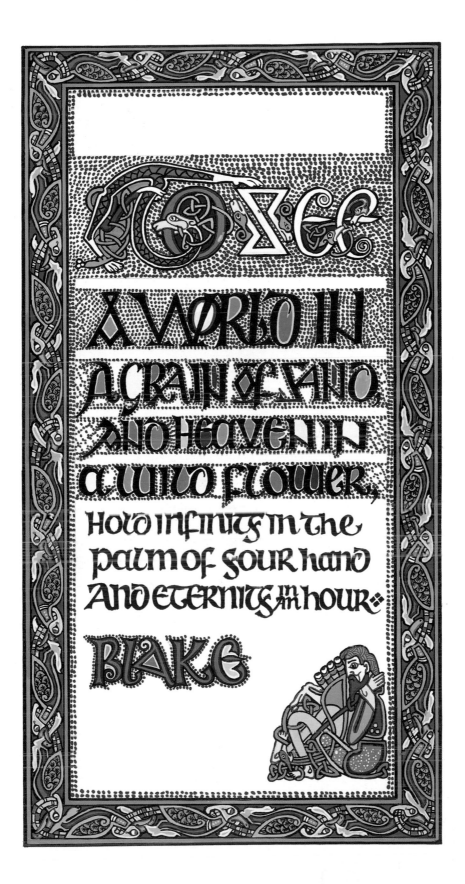

TO SEE

A WORLD IN
A GRAIN OF SAND,
AND HEAVEN IN
A WILD FLOWER,
Hold infinity in the
palm of your hand
AND ETERNITY in an hour.

BLAKE

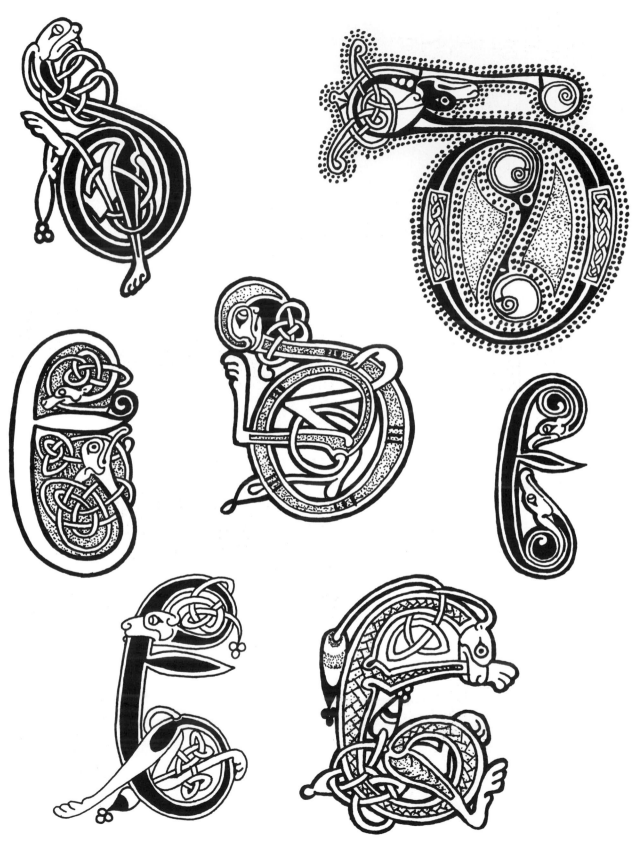

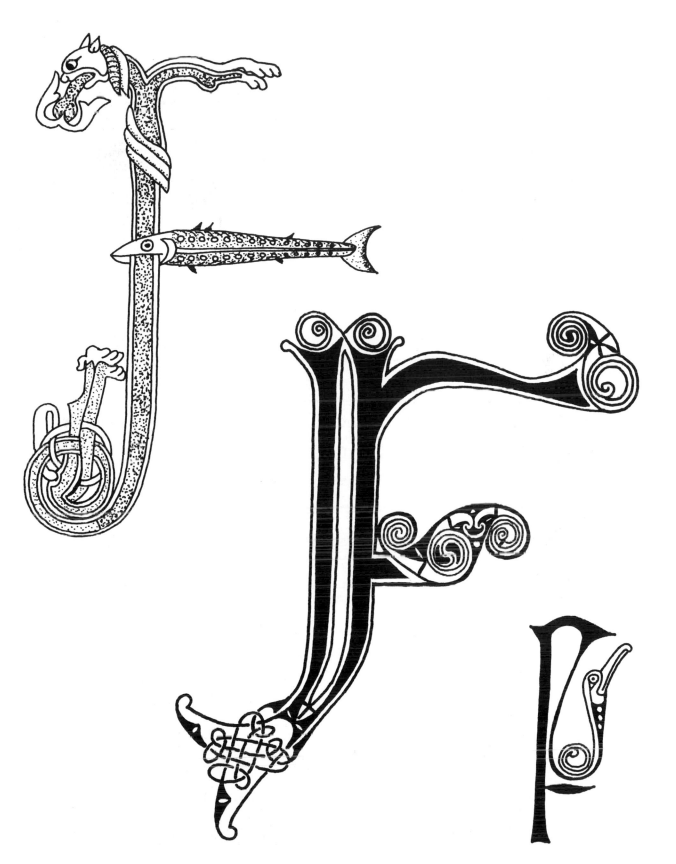

LISTEN TO THE
SILENCE
BE STILL
AND LET YOUR SOUL CATCH
UP'

Kindle this little light
on the Earth plane.

I dedicate it to the
service of the Spirit.

I guard and cherish
this light as a living symbol,
and an act of faith in the
reality of the powers of Light.

The Invocation of Light – A Celtic Prayer

Opposite: *text by Bill Westwood, Bishop of Peterborough,*
on BBC Radio's Thought for Today

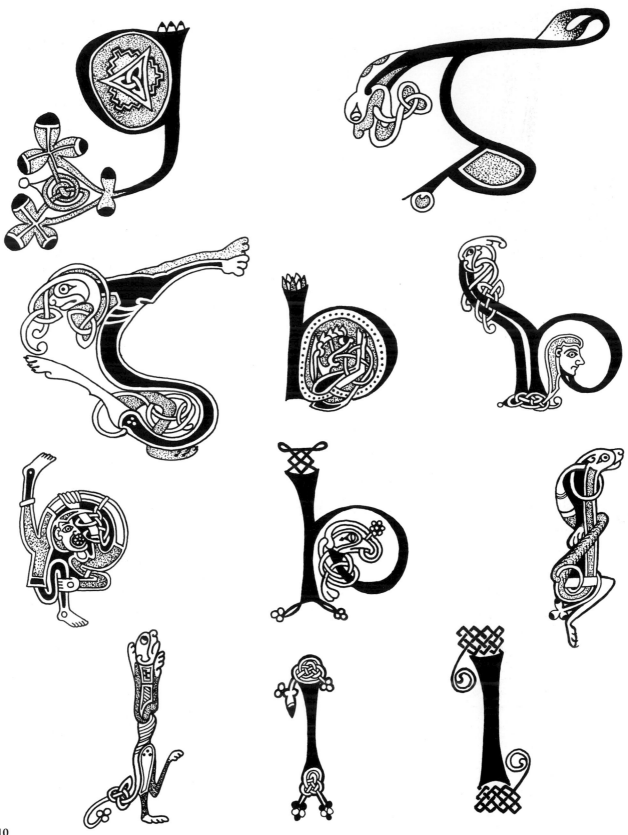

111

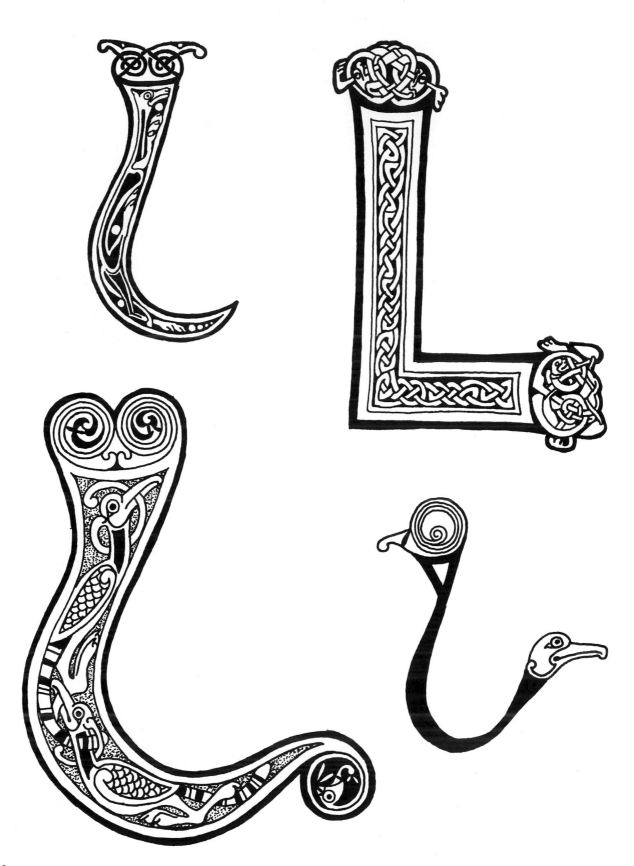

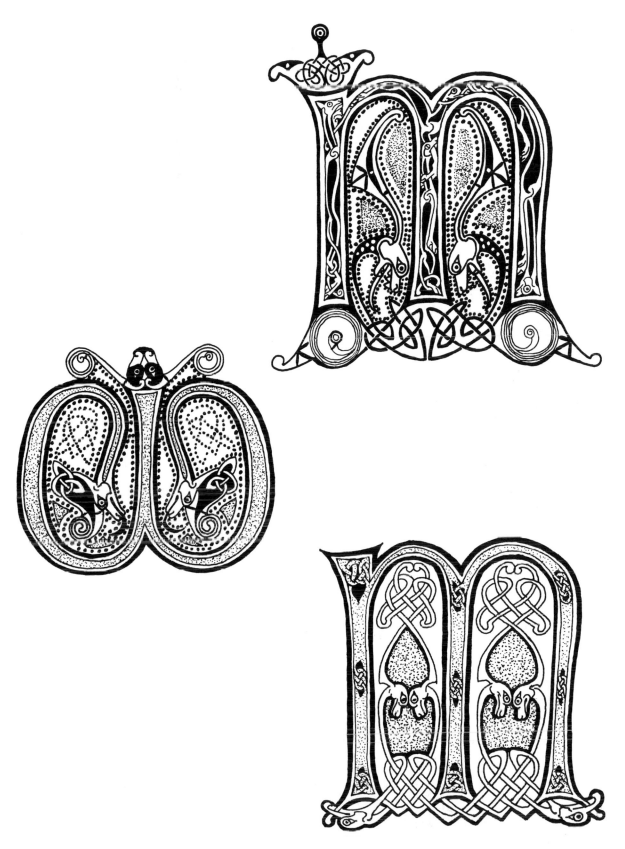

115

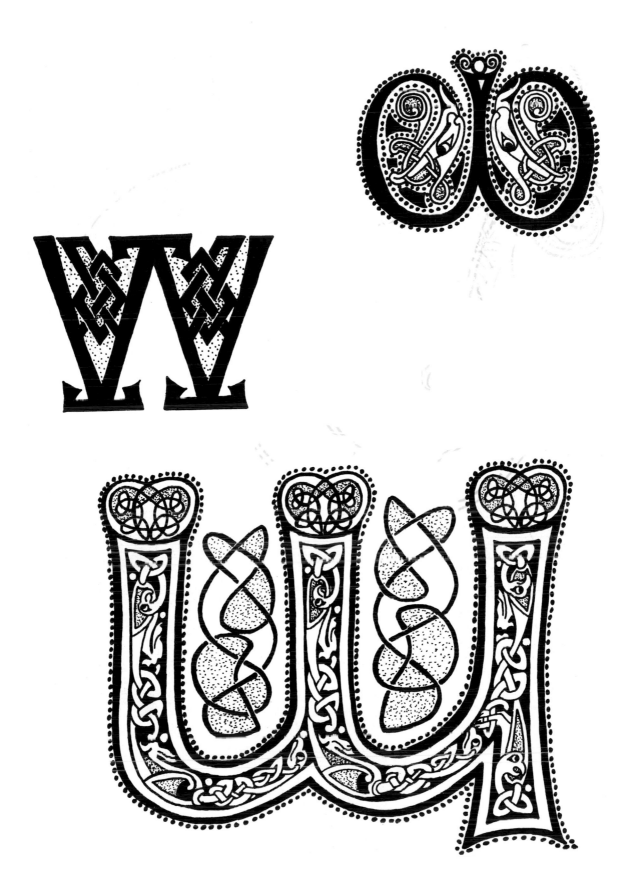

DESIGNS AND REFERENCES

The designs for the book are from the various sources listed below, reproduced as close to the originals as my skill will allow or adapted so that they may be more useful to the craftsman.

The Book of Durrow, fifth to sixth century
The Book of Kells, sixth to seventh century
The Book of Lindisfarne, seventh century
The Book of St Chad, seventh to eighth century

Within the confines of the book I was unable to do full justice to some larger areas – especially the more pagan art form, stories and legends.

Further sources:

Bain, George, *Celtic Art: The Methods of Construction*, Dover 1973.
Davis, Courtney, *The Celtic Art of Courtney Davis*, Spirit of Celtia 1985.
Matthews, John, *Fionn MacCumhail – Champion of Ireland*, Firebird Books 1988.
Matthews, John & Stewart, Bob, *Warriors of Arthur*, Blandford Press 1987.
Newark, Tim, *Celtic Warriors*, Blandford Press 1986.
Pure, Jill, *The Mystic Spiral*, Thames & Hudson 1974.
Sharkey, John, *Celtic Mysteries*, Thames & Hudson 1975.
Stewart, Bob, *Cuchulainn – Hound of Ulster*, Firebird Books 1988.
Stewart, R. J., (ed.), *The Book of Merlin*, Blandford Press 1987.
 Merlin and Woman, Blandford Press 1988.

Lighting one
candle with
another's
flame.....
at dusk in Spring,
the same, yet not
the same.   Basho

INDEX

Page numbers of illustrations are in *italics*